VICTORY OVER OPPRESSION

How To Find Yourself
after Losing Yourself

Jamez Morris

Copyright © 2022 Jamez Morris

All rights reserved.

ISBN:979-8-218-017361

DEDICATION

I dedicate this book to my younger self and to the woman I have become. To any other woman who has striven to find herself again after getting neat in life. I honor and admire you for doing the work it takes to become you.

Table Of Contents

Acknowledgments 1

Introduction 4

1 - My Upbringing 7

2 - Caught Me By Surprise 19

3 - Steals, Kill And Destroy 28

4 - Keep Your Eyes On Your Vision 38

5 - Dying Before My Eyes 44

6 - Moves Towards Purpose 56

7 - Life Must Go On 64

About The Author 88

VICTORY OVER OPPRESSION

ACKNOWLEDGMENTS

To my one true source of my strength, sovereignty, love, and patience: Thank you for walking hand in hand with me, talking with me, and loving me.

Special thanks to all the prayer warriors that stood in the gaps to pray with me and for me. As for my family and dear friends, thanks for enduring and embracing this journey called "Life"

VICTORY OVER OPPRESSION

with me in the ways you all know-how. Special thanks to Charles Williamson, my confidant, my biggest supporter and finance' for the endless support and encouragement in seeing this to the end and not letting me give up to my son, Ja'Kobi Williamson, for being my strength, my heart, my smiles in human form. I pray that you will read this ine day and be proud of mommy. To my writing coach Dennard for assisting me in carrying out the vison and writing partner Zana Kenjar for not only being my writing partner but becoming my friend in the

VICTORY OVER OPPRESSION

process. I love you all to life and there is nothing you can do about it.

VICTORY OVER OPPRESSION

INTRODUCTION

Life for me has not been an easy journey, and sometimes, I found myself not knowing if I was going or coming but I kept going. You asked how I kept going when I didn't know the direction, I was going in. The key is to just keep walking forward and not backwards with your head up. It is better to walk towards a purpose than to go back into your past. Along the way, I found that things may not always make sense and you may not always get the apology or closure you think you deserve but it is okay to

VICTORY OVER OPPRESSION

make peace with it for the better of yourself and know that you can be the person you expected out of other people. Your past is gone but today is a day that you can make count for a better tomorrow. Through the thoughts, memories, feelings, and instructions, I have written poems to capture the moments of my childhood growing up.

You're the first I decide to fully share them with. My prayer is that you learn what you can and what you need to from my story

VICTORY OVER OPPRESSION

as you are writing your own. Let my story be a guide when you are feeling lost and confused. If you are looking for permission to give up, this is not the story for you but if you need a reason to keep going, here it is.

VICTORY OVER OPPRESSION

1
MY UPBRINGING

VICTORY OVER OPPRESSION

"If you get up in the morning and think the future is going to be better, it is a bright day. Otherwise, it's not."

Elon Musk

VICTORY OVER OPPRESSION

I come from a single-parent household where I was raised with my mom and three sisters. Me, being the third oldest amongst my siblings, I watched my mom work day in and day out to provide for my sisters and I while my oldest sister looked after us. I would always say, my mom had us all at a young age so she was growing up with us. Education was a very big deal in my mom's house. She made sure we did well in school and knew how to behave outside her presents. Even on the day we weren't feeling good, my mom would always tell us to go to school and at least try, but if you get there and still not feeling well, call me from the

VICTORY OVER OPPRESSION

nurse's office. TO this day, i show up even when i am not okay and at least try. My mom was all I had, and I looked to her for everything. She was a miracle worker in my eyes because I never went without and did not feel like I was missing out on anything.

Even though my father was absent most of my childhood. I watched as most of my friends growing up had two parents in their homes and they all treated me as their own, so I didn't feel like I was missing anything.

VICTORY OVER OPPRESSION

It wasn't until my mom started taking me to visit him in prison that I wanted to get to know him. We shared the same name with only one letter being different, so that was our bond within itself. My relationship with my dad was short-lived after he came home and him and my mom didn't work out once he was released from prison. It wasn't until I moved out my mom's house that I took a chance at having a father and daughter relationship with my dad. If I could be honest, I didn't learn how a man was supposed to treat me from my dad, I went through a few trials

VICTORY OVER OPPRESSION

and errors for that but I did know what it felt like to call someone dad. My childhood was centered around survival more than it was love but it molded me into the person I am today.

Every mistake I made, came with a good cursing or a whooping and the only explanation I got was that I'm doing this because I love you, but in my young mind, that was not the love I needed.

Despite, I lived a normal childhood. I was the clumsy, mild manner, sneaky, but yet resilient child my mom had. I always

VICTORY OVER OPPRESSION

developed faster than my age and was shy about it. My mom never had to worry about me staying on top of my schoolwork because I did that on my own and she knew if the teacher was calling her that someone had to mess with me first. I was a timid, yet full of life child that always kept the peace around the house. I didn't like confrontation and always tried to do right by those around me. Growing up, I struggled to feel accepted or that I belong because I always went against the grain and did not think no was an answer but a chance to prove myself. Thinking back

VICTORY OVER OPPRESSION

on it, I didn't care to be seated at other's tables, but I rather created my own. I remember feeling like nobody understood me better than my sisters and God, of course. If I could speak to my younger self, I would say "allow yourself some grace as your grow and glow through life. It is okay not to know the ending result but continue to embrace life as it comes, and overtime things will unfold and work out for your good. I wouldn't change anything about it except being more patience with my growth. I understood now that my mom did the best with what she knew

VICTORY OVER OPPRESSION

how and the tools she was given. I always knew she loved her

girls, and she would go to war about us and back about us, but

tough love is how she showed it.

VICTORY OVER OPPRESSION

WHO AM I?
(PERSONAL POEM)

Did the person I used to be still here, or did she die? Lord speak

to me, who am I?

I used to be a nice, not all so mean, Lord what happened to me

now that I'm 13?

Is it just I got tired of holding everything in and it's all coming

out; I used to not scream nor shout?

VICTORY OVER OPPRESSION

I used to let people take advantage of me, but that has changed and now that I'm older my attitude has rearranged.

I guess the person I've become to be is who God has wanted me to be, so until he calls upon my name, I am going to be the person I am. I am going to be me.

If you want to get to know me, don't be afraid. I might look mean but that's on the outside, get to know me in the inside and maybe we could become friends.

VICTORY OVER OPPRESSION

I could wear a halo and it could turn into fire horns: some may

think my attitude has died and reborn,

I gave you a little warning of who I am so don't be surprised if

you get looked at with my evil eyes. And if you don't meet me

before died, I'm telling you who I am.

If you have any questions about me, ask me, I'll answer. I'm

not ashamed of my name, Jamez Shun Morris

2
CAUGHT ME BY SURPRISE

VICTORY OVER OPPRESSION

LIFE AS IT COMES
(Personal poem)

You never know what may come at you. Only God knows and always knew. Life is too short not to forgive and forget so why should you regret it. You can't change the past so stop writing checks that you can't cash. Hold on to the good and bad memories that live within you and learn from the bad choices that you choose to make.

VICTORY OVER OPPRESSION

You can't ever say that you did not make any mistakes in your life because everybody does. No one is perfect, no one including you.

Things come at you when you least expect them. It can be good or bad but all you can do is move on and accept it.

Keep moving forward in life. Don't give up on yourself now. I know you're asking how. How can I smile when I've been hurt so many times and God didn't even warn me? He didn't send me

VICTORY OVER OPPRESSION

no signs. when you're stuck between two dilemmas and don't know what to pick or choose. Just stop and think everything through. You can't go back in time so just *Live Life as It Comes* until the end of your lifeline.

It was during winter break of my freshman year in high school that I went in to get two of my wisdom removed. I was extremely nervous because the dentist was my least favorite and I feared for the worst. I counted to five and next thing you know, I was

VICTORY OVER OPPRESSION

waking up to leave. Leaving the dentist that day felt like a blur. It was almost like I was operating outside of my body. I was so drowsy that I fell asleep soon as I got in the back seat of my mom's car. From that day forward, I was sleeping more than I was awake. I only wake up to get my daily dose of prescribed medicine to help with the pain and nausea from the extraction. I barely had an appetite and when I did eat, I would only eat strawberries and bananas sliced up and drink juice.

VICTORY OVER OPPRESSION

A couple of weeks went past, and it was time to return to school and my mom notices something about me was off. I couldn't talk, didn't eat much, and was not interested in coming out of the room. My mom would take me out to eat and I would be so embarrassed that I would stare at the floor as I walked. At the time, it was unclear to me what happened to me. My mom and my sisters were the only people I was comfortable being around because I know they wouldn't let anything happen to me but I knew they were just as confused as I was.

VICTORY OVER OPPRESSION

I wouldn't look in the mirror as I always felt dirty and ugly. My mom joked and said, you are going to have to start paying the water bill." I didn't weigh much, to begin with, but my pounds started falling off more and more.

My mom took me to my primary care doctor to get answers. They told her I was fine, but she knew it had to be more to it than that, so I ended up in the hospital. From the hospital, I just went along with the process of getting back to normal, but it seemed so far

VICTORY OVER OPPRESSION

reached. I wasn't the same person after the extraction. I didn't know the outcome of everything, but I knew I wanted to be alive to see it. Not only had my teeth been extracted but apart of me went with it. My trust for those who I believed had my best interest at heart, was gone. I did not know who to trust or if I should trust anyone to open up to about what had happened to me, so I kept quiet. I appeared as if I was okay but inside, I was breaking. I knew I was't crazy or was I stupid but how could I get others to believe me when this poison had taken over my body,

VICTORY OVER OPPRESSION

from the way I talk to the way I functioned. I knew God and I knew he was keeping me because he was allowing this to happen to me, but I wanted to experience him and I need to experience him. I would listen to *Kirk Franklin, God's property* album on repeat and that one song, "*More Than I Could Bare*." It minster to be and I began to ask God to use me as your vessel that you may receive the glory from this.

3
STEALS, KILL AND DESTROY

VICTORY OVER OPPRESSION

CASTING OUT A DRUG OVERDOSE
(Personal poem)

Doctors thought I was crazy. Mama took me to church and that's what saved me. God said it wasn't my time to go. He delivered me from a drug overdose. I was delusional, not even knowing my name, and wouldn't sleep for anything. A shut eye causes me to get an MRI on my brain. I was out of school for about a month not even wanting to pick up a spoon for lunch. In and out of the

VICTORY OVER OPPRESSION

hospital seen by different doctors and nurses. They wouldn't tell my mama anything besides giving me medicine. That's when my mama begins with the frustrated curses. Everyone was sad, puzzled not knowing what to do. My mother prayed and prayed along with a lot of others too. They prayed for me, and God took me under His wings and carried me. During that time, I thought I wasn't going to make it the devil was telling me, it's your time to go for heaven's sake. After I was healed, I lifted my hands to God and said thank you, Lord, I'm still here for us, and to give

VICTORY OVER OPPRESSION

you all the honor and glory is a must. God, how would this have ever ended, no one knows. Only you are powerful enough to Cast Out a Drug Overdose.

When all else fails, what do you do? My house mom was desperate to get me help.

She had called all the family over to the house that night and I did not want to come out of the room. What brought me out of the room was when I heard the song playing, *"My Life Is in Your*

VICTORY OVER OPPRESSION

Hands by Kirk Franklin." Suddenly, my mom thought to take me to church for prayer. Prayer changes things, right? That Wednesday, my family and I went to Bible study and the pastor agreed to pray over me after Bible study ended. It wasn't until this moment that I experience God for myself. If I could describe this moment in time in one word, it would be powerful. My mom walked me to the altar as the pastor received me and was told to stand back as they prayed for me. I did not know what to expect. Being raised in the church, I have seen people go to alter call all

VICTORY OVER OPPRESSION

the time, but never witnessed anything like I had experienced. It started off with just a simple oil rubbed across my head in the shape of a cross as those around me anointed their hands and heads as well. From there it was almost as if the enemy and God were fighting to win me over. I had so much force inside me that I began to try and run from God. As the prayer warriors around me began to pray deeper and deeper, I began to put up a fight as if I didn't want Jesus around me. I could heard the prayer warriors say, "get out of her, get out of her. Lose her, loose her." I wept,

VICTORY OVER OPPRESSION

I looked for my mom and ask if I could go to her and I was told no that the demons could get on her. I didn't understand what came over me. The oil was getting poured down my throat as the pastor grabbed and repeatedly shout out get out of her right now. I could feel a ball move from my throat to my stomach depending on where the pastor laid his hands. After a few hours, I was sat down, and asked to say "Jesus", I uttered the words softly but that was all I could say. I cried and cried as they prayed and prayed over me until one in the morning. Finally, the pastor sent me

VICTORY OVER OPPRESSION

home with oil and juice, and told my mom that I would have to release the demons either through my mouth or through my bowel movement. I went home so exhausted and drained that I just wanted to crawl under my mom and go to sleep. I never came so close to the enemy that I wanted nothing more than to defeat him. I was determined to put on a full armor of God and go to war with him. He came to kill, steal and destroy but I came to seek victory over the enemy. I always said I am a spiritual fighter not spiritually stupid. The enemy saw that I was weak and choose to

VICTORY OVER OPPRESSION

attack but I came that I may have life and life more abundantly, so I was willing to go to war with him because I experience how God fought for me on the inside and I knew with him I could not fail. I stared the enemy in the eyes until he was mad that I continued to wake up in the mornings.

I learned that if I keep showing up for myself, something good will come out of it. There were so many others prayer for me, but when I began to pray for myself, I felt the shame, the guilt, the

VICTORY OVER OPPRESSION

low-self- esteem, the confusion extract from my body. Time and time again, I had to pick myself up, out of a dark place and it started and ended with prayer and obedience. God will have us doing things that may seem crazy but if I am going to look crazy, I rather look crazy for Jesus than a fool by myself.

4
KEEP YOUR EYES ON YOUR VISION

VICTORY OVER OPPRESSION

MY WEARY EYES SHALL CARRY ON
(Personal poem)

I walk with faith although my eyes are witnessing a light tangible but, yet, so far away. I'm backed against the wall, but the God in me won't sleep. I know that He is still carrying me. My source has run out. I have nobody else to turn to cry on. No shoulders nearby. God has opened the doorways to Heaven, that sign was your clue.

VICTORY OVER OPPRESSION

I need somebody to lean on. No shoulders nearby. God said, try me, I am always here. I said God I will lean on you, father; I turned this battle over to you. My life is in your hands and Father I trust in you. I feel so alone, but I'm also strong, My Weary Eyes Shall Carry On.

Victory belongs to Jesus. Shortly after, I returned to school to finish my nineth grade year. I came back in the middle of mid-term exams, and I passed all my exams and advanced to the next

VICTORY OVER OPPRESSION

grade Returning to school that year felt like a new beginning. I did not return the same vulnerable, fearful, student that I was but I had a lot to prove and was up for the challenge. My friends embraced me and told me how much they missed me while I was out but when asked what happen, I withheld the truth and only told them I was sick. In my mind, I thought, they would think I was crazy. Who else has gone through this at my age? Who could I relate to? To protect myself, I never opened up about it to anyone that was not there to see it for themselves. There was one

VICTORY OVER OPPRESSION

friend who my mama told at that time, and I remember her coming straight off a plane coming back from Jamaica to check on me at the house. She looked at me sitting up in the bed and without any words, we both began to cry. She was my closest friend at that time, and I knew that she wouldn't judge me or share with anyone else but I felt ashamed for her to see me in such an unstable state. I didn't feel like I belong at the school or to any clicks, so I started to stand along. I would only feel comfortable when I ran into my sister at school. I started to walk

VICTORY OVER OPPRESSION

to the beat of my own drums and did things that I felt comfortable

with.

5
DYING BEFORE MY EYES

VICTORY OVER OPPRESSION

"Just as God made those little green apples" Random saying from my grandmother It was her explanation when there was none.

It was a few days away from my senior year where I thought I endured a great deal of pain thus far but the one I was facing was far more painful. I remember my mama getting the call that my grandmother was in the hospital coughing up blood.

When we arrived, the doctor told us she had lung cancer and that she had six months to live. It was February and in August my

VICTORY OVER OPPRESSION

grandmother took her final rest. It was my first time ever hearing about hospice. A place that gets you ready to die, is how I best describe it.

Even in my grandmother's dying days, she lived her life as if she owned it. She did everything she wanted to without the permission of anyone. She was very comical and loved to tell jokes and make us laugh. She spoke her mind and always stood up for what was right. My grandmother was the person that saved

VICTORY OVER OPPRESSION

me from not only myself but the mental institution where I was being detained. In her boldness and her integrity to do what was right, she could no longer sleep at night knowing she was home and I was there and my sister being sad because they were missing me so she did something about it. One night, I was rushed to the hospital after having a nervous breakdown. I began sweating as I was hallucinating, urinating on myself, and I shouted out all kinds of crazy things I can't even remember. I was so spaced out; I could not even tell you what day it was.

VICTORY OVER OPPRESSION

During this time, I grew very frustrated that I had not returned to school and been able to function on my own. From the hospital, I was baker acted into a mental facility where I was being held for further evaluation. I was devasted. Mentally and physically, I died that day. Going through the evaluation process, the counselors were telling my mom that I would go to school there and receive a special diploma and wouldn't see my family as much. That was basically going to be home temporarily where my family would have to visit me.

VICTORY OVER OPPRESSION

That night, before my mom left me, she said; do not let them give you any medicine. No medicine was all I could hear my mom telling me. I couldn't sleep the whole time I was in there until I grabbed a Bible and slept with it on my chest and fell asleep. I felt like I was an experiment and that this was going to be my new home. I missed my sisters and just being a normal kid but that was all snatched away from me. Everyone had given up on me until my grandmother came after forty-eight hours of being there and demanded that the facility release me. She came and

VICTORY OVER OPPRESSION

would not take no for answer. She said; this is not a place for my granddaughter and I am taking her away from here. My prayer was answered, I thought but then, once I left, I thought I had done something wrong, and they were going to come pick me up and take me back. My grandmother assured me that I was safe and never going back there again. My mother took me to another mental facility to get a second opinion.

VICTORY OVER OPPRESSION

Luckily, they did not find enough reasoning to keep me, and I was free to go home.

Three years later, is when we found out my grandmother only had six months to live, and she was dying before our eyes. I saw how my grandmother went from working a nine to five, living on her own, and moving to the beat of her own drums to having to have an oxygen tank everywhere she went. It had gotten so bad that my mom had asked me to spend the night with my

VICTORY OVER OPPRESSION

grandmother to keep an eye on her. While there, I took full advantage of the time with my grandmother, I remember her telling me, Mez, you have to stop stressing or you're going to kill yourself. Grandma loves you." Whenever I find myself stressed, I could hear my grandmother's words speak softly in my ears.

I wrote this poem shortly after my grandmother spoke these words to me. I hold them near and dear as I maneuver through life.

VICTORY OVER OPPRESSION

STRESS ME, YOU WILL NOT
(Personal poem)

I can't get a break, there isn't enough hours in the day for me. As time whines down, I suddenly get frustrated and angry.

Sleep slowly comes down on me and I've yet to catch a break, my day begins to deteriorate.

I put a hundred percent effort into all that I do.

VICTORY OVER OPPRESSION

I know that all of my efforts will pay off a little now and some

later… my tolerance of patience is running by the few.

I'm not even supposed to be rhyming in this poem, at least, that's

what I told myself I wouldn't do.

It's hard for me not to when the thoughts just flow on through.

Tough soul of mine weakens and bows down to help.

"I can't do, I can't do it" that demon wept.

Street me. you will not, I won't allow you to.

VICTORY OVER OPPRESSION

Mez. Laugh in the face of this demon. I dare you to.

Encouraging myself is what it will take. Motivating myself through faith and prayer is what is going to cause this yoke to break.

I come out on top, "Stress Me You Will Not"

6
MOVES TOWARDS PURPOSE

VICTORY OVER OPPRESSION

"In order to become a well-rounded person, you must first step out of the box and shape of the edges."

Jamez Morris

VICTORY OVER OPPRESSION

Here's Where I Start

The more I repeated that, the more I believed in it and accepted my shortcomings as I allowed myself to grow from them. My life was never smooth sailing as I continued to get thrown off course time and time again. One thing that I always had a clear understanding of was, the will of God over my life and I kept my eyes on Him despite the situation. The hardest part about writing this book was having to relive the moments that inspired it. For

VICTORY OVER OPPRESSION

me to move forward with my life, I had to make a choice to heal what had me bound for so long. I had to remind myself time and time again to get out of my own way and let the Holy Spirit have His way in me. It was no longer about me and my story but the test that I encounter that later became my testimony.

After high school, I moved out of my mother's house to go live with my boyfriend at the time thinking I was ready to be on my own while pursuing my A. A degree. I soon found out that-- that

VICTORY OVER OPPRESSION

was not the smartest idea. I was slowly losing myself in him. I Turned into a person he wanted me to be, by drinking, wearing clothes that were revealing, and allowing him to treat me like a nobody. He would call me out by my name and even choked me one time. There was where I drew the line. As he was choking me, I told him I have to leave the place one day but he will not be the one to kill me, that was the day I realized, that he was not the guy for me and moved back into my mother's house to finish obtaining my A.A degree at Valencia. It took me two years to

VICTORY OVER OPPRESSION

realize that but I had to leave well enough along to get back focused and limit the unnecessary detraction. It did not matter who I had to eliminate in order to get the job done, they had to go. I struggled to love myself after that but then I started to see how far I came without him and kept moving forward. The words I spoke to him, spoke back to me years and years later, and that was my driving force. I knew that it was a reason God let me live through this that was supposed to take me out. I had a purpose that he wanted me to fulfill and I was determined to do just that.

VICTORY OVER OPPRESSION

A program that was supposed to take two years took me two and half years but with perseverance, I received my A. An A in Social Sciences. I went from being told I would receive a special diploma to receiving a full-ride scholarship to my dream school and two other scholarships to further my education graduating high school in 2012. Due to the fear of failing and losing who I thought was the love of my life I decided to stay locally and attended Valencia Community College. I didn't stop there. After receiving my A.A degree. I got accepted into Florida

VICTORY OVER OPPRESSION

Agricultural and Mechanical University in Tallahassee Florida but missed my chances of starting classes the first time around. I end up in jail. Me, being an honor roll student, who stayed to herself and didn't cause any trouble ended up in handcuffs. It all happened so fast that it took me a while to wrap my mind around it.

7
LIFE MUST GO ON

VICTORY OVER OPPRESSION

"I just wanted to be free, free of what had me bound for so long."

Jamez Morris

VICTORY OVER OPPRESSION

LIFE MUST GO ON

Here I am. Having to sit down in my tracks. Where do I go from here? How do I move on when I can barely move at all? How can I focus on my future when I am stuck in limbo? I'll tell you what, I have plenty of time to think about it now. It is mind over matter, and now, I am figuring out exactly what that means. It's coming to the realization that I am not my past, my failures, my mistakes, or my own expectations but far beyond all of that. I must first

VICTORY OVER OPPRESSION

apologize to myself for the way I have treated myself. Then, apologize to myself for the way I let others treat me. How could I carry on in turmoil for so long? How could I not see myself in the same light that God created me in? I blocked out the truth about who God said I am and ignored the instructions He gave me. Now, as I open my heart, my mind, and my soul up to the will God has in my life, I walk intentionally on purpose. I am not sure what all I am destined to fulfill but from this point on, I will live my life accordingly. I will go wherever God leads me. So far, I

VICTORY OVER OPPRESSION

love it better in this place. Happy. Free of bondage with a leveled head and a willingness to do God's will. Life must go on.

It took me to go to jail to come to reach this level of maturity.

What was supposed to be a family outing to go watch fireworks for the fourth of July ended up being a day that changed my life forever. I was exhausted, drained, and stressed to the point, I called out that day to rest but after taking down the guilt trip of missing family time I decided to go to the event with my family.

VICTORY OVER OPPRESSION

What matters to me the most at that time was getting accepted into Florida A and M University. I had spent countless hours making sure I had everything required to get in despite the challenges that I faced. That fear that I wasn't smart enough, overpowered and created worry that didn't need to be there. I had no support to help with the process and it was the first time I would be away from home, so I wanted to make sure I had money saved to get me started. With that in the back of my mind, I worked full time and helped my mother out with bills. All my

VICTORY OVER OPPRESSION

hard work had paid off and I received my acceptance letter to get into FAMU. It was a breath of fresh air but the wind got knocked out of me before I can fully grasp it.

Once we arrived at the event known as Red Hot and Boom, I remember being so tired that I could barely think straight. I told my family that I sat on the wall as they kept walking around. I sat there and all the feelings of my past caught up to me and I got so

VICTORY OVER OPPRESSION

tired of it consuming me that I released a big punch in the air and almost hit a security guard in the face.

Don't resist, don't resist, was all I heard as my face was on the ground with my hands behind my back and a knee in my neck. I was escorted in front of a crowd of people but all I could think about was how sorry I was for displeasing God. I kept repeating how sorry I was and asked for my mom.

VICTORY OVER OPPRESSION

That night, after hours of booking, I was placed in a cell myself.

It was dark, loud, and cold. I centered my thoughts on crying out

to God until I fell asleep. Even in my mess, it was crazy to feel

God's presence. I was certain that He was disappointed in me but

He still was keeping me.

I was charged with disturbing the peace and disturbance without

violence and was released after forty hours before my bond was

revoked due to my mom's discrepancy of not feeling comfortable

VICTORY OVER OPPRESSION

with the amount of freedom I had. She was scared that I was mentally stable to function outside of jail and needed professional help, so she turned me back in. Being that I was in jail, I was withheld from starting at FAMU that semester. All my hard work was thrown down the drain… I thought to myself as I was being held in confinement. I would only get out of my cell long enough to shower and the only way I could tell the difference between night and day is through a very small window.

VICTORY OVER OPPRESSION

God had got me exactly where He needed me. Along in a room by myself where He was the only person I could depend on. I leaned not to my own understanding and knew that His plans were far greater than mine. After seven days of being in confinement I was released into general population where I would be around other inmates and earn the privilege of going outside for recreation time. As soon as I walked into the mod with other women, another inmate called me over and welcomed me in. I told her how I ended up in there and from that day forward

VICTORY OVER OPPRESSION

she encouraged me to continue the work I started after I was released from that place. It was her belief in me that gave me something to look forward to when I got out.

Twenty days later, I was released. I had lost everything. My job, my car insurance, my acceptance into the school, and even myself. I didn't know where I belong or where to start but I knew the vision that I was given and I had to see it come to pass. I immediately contacted FAMU to get my chance to prove myself

VICTORY OVER OPPRESSION

again and become a rattler at their school. My godmother allowed me to stay with her for the time being until I sorted things out. She was always in my corner, giving me love in any way she could. Her talks gave me the greatest motivation and she would always have me read a daily devotion each morning before starting my day. I got reacquainted with a guy that I met a guy at my job before I got fired, that would turn out to be my biggest supporter and one of the greatest bonds I had this far. I was given a second chance with FAMU and got accepted again. with all the

VICTORY OVER OPPRESSION

money given out of his pocket, a wing, and a prayer I was sent on my way to better my future.

I received my Batchelor's in Psychology with a minor in Criminal Justice in 2017 and today I am on my fifth quarter of my master's program for School Counseling. I am now engaged with a six- month-old son. Life will go on, but will you carry on the same way and pity yourself or would you rise above it and do something to change it.

VICTORY OVER OPPRESSION

FOOTSTONES TO VICTORY

VICTORY OVER OPPRESSION

*Accept mistakes
as lessons learned*

VICTORY OVER OPPRESSION

Don't run away from correction; embrace it, cherish and use it as needed

VICTORY OVER OPPRESSION

*Pray until
you feel better*

VICTORY OVER OPPRESSION

Don't expect you out of other people. Show them how to live

VICTORY OVER OPPRESSION

Seek God out for direction when you don't know which way to go

VICTORY OVER OPPRESSION

Forgive yourself just as much as you forgive others but forgive

VICTORY OVER OPPRESSION

Speak highly of yourself, think highly of yourself

VICTORY OVER OPPRESSION

Stop beating yourself up so much, life does that enough on its own

VICTORY OVER OPPRESSION

Laugh in the Face of Anger. Smile in the face of fear and Love in the face of Hatred

ABOUT THE AUTHOR
Victory Over Oppression

It's time to get up sis and get back to you.

Have you struggled with finding yourself after experiencing shortcomings or obstacles? Are you having a hard time accepting this thing you cannot change in your past that prevents you from your future?

As a woman who has jumped many hurdles throughout her life, I just want to be that light in your life to help you do the same. I

VICTORY OVER OPPRESSION

know what it is like to not know where to begin to pick up the piece of your life and move forward but I am here to attest to it. I wrote this book to show you that mistakes will be made but they don't have to define you. There is life after someone has done you wrong. Sometimes, you will find that you have not only forgiven others in the process, but you have forgiven yourself as well.

VICTORY OVER OPPRESSION

Taking that next step after getting up from being knockdown isn't easy but it is very possible. I overcame a lot of adversities to be able to live to the title of a mother, a fiancé, a student, a sister, and a daughter. From one woman to the next, I encourage you to get up sister, and get back to yourself.

Jamez Morris is a college graduate with a Bachelor's in Psychology with a minor in Criminal Justice who is currently pursuing her master's in School Counseling. She is a mother of

VICTORY OVER OPPRESSION

a baby boy and a devoted fiancé. She loves to inspire, encourage and uplift those around her.

www.ingramcontent.com/pod-product-compliance
Lightning Source LLC
Chambersburg PA
CBHW071226160426
43196CB00012B/2427